Meeting Prayers

Philip A. Verhalen

Editor

THE LITURGICAL PRESS
Collegeville, Minnesota

www.litpress.org

Cover design by Ann Blattner. Photo by Marie Docher, PhotoAlto.

1   2   3   4   5   6   7   8   9

ISBN 0-8146-2772-2

To
Lay Ministers
of
Our Global Village

Contents

Acknowledgments

The Scripture quotations are from the New Revised Standard Version Bible, Catholic edition, © 1989 by the Division of Christian Education of the National Council of Churches of Christ in the USA. Used by permission. All rights reserved.

Editors of Conari Press, *Random Acts of Kindness* (Emeryville, Calif.: Conari Press, 1993) 20, 27, 47, 53.

Anonymous, "A Prayer for Wisdom," *Challenge 2000,* ed. Mark Link (Allen, Tex.: Tabor Publishers, 1993) 79.

Mark Link, *Vision 2000* (Allen, Tex.: Tabor Publishers, 1992) 51.

A Treasury of Great Poems, vol. 2, ed. Louis Untermeyer (New York: Simon and Schuster, 1955). Excerpts included in this work are: Matthew Arnold, "Quiet Work" (p. 923); Robert Browning, "Pippa Passes" (p. 861); Gerard Manley Hopkins, "God's Grandeur" (pp. 978–9); Henry Wadsworth Longfellow, "Nature" (p. 809); William Wordsworth, "Lines, Composed a Few Miles Above Tintern Abbey" (p. 640); Sara Teasdale, "Let It Be Forgotten" (p. 1118); Alfred Tennyson, "Oh Yet We Trust" (p. 827), "Ulysses" (p. 829), "Flower in the Crannied Wall" (p. 837).

Anthony de Mello, *The Song of the Bird* (Gujaret, India: Sahitya Prakash Anand, 1982) 4–5, 46–7.

Elizabeth Roberts and Elias Amidon, eds., *Earth Prayers* (San Francisco: HarperCollins Publishers, 1991) 118.

The Oxford Book of Prayers, ed. George Appleton (New York: Oxford University Press, 1985) 125, 159, 172, 366, 367.

Christina G. Rossetti, "A Christmas Carol," *Selected Poems,* ed. C. H. Sisson (Manchester: Carcanet Press Ltd., 1984) 126, 127.

Thomas Merton, "Carol," *The Collected Poems of Thomas Merton* (New York: New Directions, 1977).

I wish to extend my personal thanks to the editors of The Liturgical Press for allowing me to compile this book of prayers. Much of the material in this book is taken from *Prayers for the Classroom,* published by The Liturgical Press, Collegeville, Minnesota.

All personal efforts are ultimately community efforts. I wish to thank quite humbly the many persons who have supported me in this endeavor: John Olivier; Mary Lou Hertzberg; Lynne Davis; Bob and Helen Batie; Kathleen Schlumpf; Marian Leonard; Tom Gross Shader; Tim Milnes; Rita Kowatts; Darrell and Lucy Reeck; Walt and Margie Babb; Walt and Donna Abel; Jim Goodwin, s.j.; Ray and Marian Malonson; Dorothy and Phil Brandt; Dale Turner; my brothers, Charlie and Jim, and Jim's wonderful wife, Flo; my younger sister, Rosie; and many others at Bellarmine Prep in Tacoma. Moreover, I wish to thank Fred and Polly at TypeRight for placing the text in an orderly form. To all of you, my affection and thanks.

Introduction

Coming together for a meeting is a community-building work in itself. In general, many values unite the group, but a particular agenda can point out clearly how many divisions exist within the same group. A prayer at the beginning of a meeting, and when suitable at the end of a meeting, clarifies how united we are in our most important spiritual values. Prayer draws us out of our individual agendas to reflect on the larger, more encompassing agenda that works for the honor of God and the building up of God's kingdom. I hope these prayers will encourage all members of the organization using them to reflect upon the disarming graciousness of our God.

When I lead the prayer at our faculty sessions, I always begin by having classical music playing softly in the background. Many CDs are available that contain splendid adagios and parts of the second movements of memorable symphonies and concertos by the great masters. If the meeting is particularly critical, I rely on this atmosphere to help us move to an awareness of the presence of God. Strangely enough, as the meeting begins I become aware of the promise of Jesus: "For where two or three are gathered in my name, I am there among them" (Matt 18:20).

Prayers for Each Month of the Year

January Prayers

New Year, New Resolve

Kindness

Theodore Isaac Rubin remarked: "Kindness is more important than wisdom, and the recognition of this is the beginning of wisdom." Yet, there are some of us too busy with our developing projects and ascending careers to look to the work of kindness and the world of love. We see so often the world only as an opportunity for mastering all of the forces for growth other than those forces growing out of our deepest selves. Chardin said: "Some day, after we have mastered the winds, the waves, the tides and gravity we shall harness the energies of love. Then, for the second time in the history of the world, the human race will have discovered fire."

—*Random Acts of Kindness*

NEW YEAR, NEW RESOLVE

God's Ways

As we turn to God in prayer, often we wonder if God really understands our needs and aspirations. Then we catch ourselves, and recall our sense of a wise, all-loving creator. Isaiah 55 consoles us with an awareness of how different from God's perceptions are our perceptions of life. In Isaiah God explains:

> For my thoughts are not your thoughts,
>   nor are your ways my ways, says the LORD.
> For as the heavens are higher than the earth,
>   so are my ways higher than your ways
>   and my thoughts than your thoughts.
>
> For as the rain and the snow come down from
>   heaven,
>   and do not return there until they have watered the
>   earth,
> making it bring forth and sprout,
>   giving seed to the sower and bread to the eater,
> so shall my word be that goes out from my mouth;
>   it shall not return to me empty,
> but it shall accomplish that which I purpose,
>   and succeed in the thing for which I sent it.

—Isaiah 55:8-11

A Prayer for Wisdom

Here is another famous prayer of petition by our good friend "Anonymous":

I asked for health,
that I might do greater things:
I was given infirmity,
that I might do better things. . . .
I asked for riches,
that I might be happy:
I was given poverty,
that I might be wise. . . .
I asked for power,
that I might have the praise of other persons:
I was given weakness,
that I might feel the need of God. . . .
I asked for all things,
that I might enjoy life:
I was given life,
that I might enjoy all things. . . .
I got nothing I asked for,
but everything I hoped for.
Almost despite myself,
my unspoken prayers were answered,
I am among all persons most richly blessed.

—Anonymous

NEW YEAR, NEW RESOLVE

Faith

Faith is our response to the revelation of God. How well the Jews sensed their closeness to God; how appreciative they were of their faith!

> Now faith is the assurance of things hoped for, the conviction of things not seen. Indeed, by faith our ancestors received approval. By faith we understand that the worlds were prepared by the word of God, so that what is seen was made from things that are not visible.
>
> By faith Abraham obeyed when he was called to set out for a place that he was to receive as an inheritance; and he set out, not knowing where he was going. By faith he stayed for a time in the land he had been promised, as in a foreign land, living in tents, as did Isaac and Jacob, who were heirs with him of the same promise. For he looked forward to the city that has foundations, whose architect and builder is God.
>
> —Hebrews 11:1-3, 8-10

February Prayers

*Winter Crisp and Warm Fires
for Heart and Hearth*

WINTER CRISP AND WARM FIRES FOR HEART AND HEARTH

Pass the Torch

Robert Bellah in *Habits of the Heart* reminds us that today, unfortunately, we have moved from community awareness to individual awareness. We are told, taught, and cajoled to value self above community. Well, we need to move beyond the classic argument of what is more important—the life of the community or the life of the individual. For now, we will pray over the quote of George Bernard Shaw.

I am of the opinion that my life belongs to the community, and as long as I live, it is my privilege to do for it whatever I can. I want to be thoroughly used up when I die, for the harder I work, the more I live. Life is no "brief candle" to me. It is a sort of splendid torch which I have got hold of for a moment, and I want to make it burn as brightly as possible before handing it on to future generations.

—George Bernard Shaw,
as quoted in *Random Acts of Kindness*, 27

WINTER CRISP AND WARM FIRES FOR HEART AND HEARTH

Strength for the Weary

As youth we feel we have unlimited energy. Yet, we too grow tired and seek out a time of rest. Isaiah points out that God renews our strength and often gives us strength and endurance that surprises us!

> Have you not known? Have you not heard?
> The LORD is the everlasting God,
>   the Creator of the ends of the earth.
> He does not faint or grow weary;
>   his understanding is unsearchable.
> He gives power to the faint,
>   and strengthens the powerless.
> Even youths will faint and be weary,
>   and the young will fall exhausted;
> but those who wait for the LORD shall renew their
>   strength,
>   they shall mount up with wings like eagles,
> they shall run and not be weary,
>   they shall walk and not faint.

—Isaiah 40:28-31

WINTER CRISP AND WARM FIRES FOR HEART AND HEARTH

An Indian Prayer

The North American native possessed a deep spirituality much to the surprise of the exploitative immigrants from Europe. Somehow, even in the acceptance of Christianity, a deep spirituality tied to their pre-Christian ancestors remains.

O Great Spirit,
Whose voice I hear in the winds,
And whose breath gives life to all the world, hear
me!
I am small and weak, I need your strength and
wisdom.
Let Me Walk in Beauty, and make my eyes ever
behold the red and purple sunset.
Make My Hands respect the things you have made
and my ears sharp to hear your voice.
Make Me Wise so that I may understand the things
you have brought my people.
Let Me Learn the lessons you have hidden in every
leaf and rock.
I Seek Strength, not to be greater than my brother,
but to fight my greatest enemy—myself.
Make Me Always Ready to come to you with clean
hands and straight eyes.
So When Life Fades, as the fading sunset, my spirit
may come to you without shame.

God Described as Father, Son, and Spirit—Helping Us

Much of what we are is hidden. For years it is hidden from ourselves. In time, we discover our hidden gifts, then it remains hidden only from others who fail to call upon us in a spirit of charity. Once the Spirit of God lives in us we are able to serve God effectively by reaching out to our neighbor. The Letter to the Ephesians gives us this Trinitarian meditation.

For this reason I bow my knees before the Father, from whom every family in heaven and on earth takes its name. I pray that, according to the riches of his glory, he may grant that you may be strengthened in your inner being with power through his Spirit, and that Christ may dwell in your hearts through faith, as you are being rooted and grounded in love. I pray that you may have the power to comprehend, with all the saints, what is the breadth and length and height and depth, and to know the love of Christ that surpasses knowledge, so that you may be filled with all the fullness of God.

—Ephesians 3:14-19

March Prayers

Lent and Lapsed Time

LENT AND LAPSED TIME

Forgiveness

Connected with the funeral liturgy is the remarkable Psalm 130, called "From the Depths." The psalmist's prayer for God's forgiveness is readily understood as available to the faith-filled Jew. Repeating this psalm once again, we have yet one more opportunity to reflect on the role of forgiveness in God's life but also in the believer's life as he or she is expected to forgive others to certify the faith rooted in our forgiving God.

Out of the depths I cry to you, O LORD.
 Lord, hear my voice!
Let your ears be attentive
 to the voice of my supplications!

If you, O LORD, should mark iniquities,
 Lord, who could stand?
But there is forgiveness with you,
 so that you may be revered.

I wait for the LORD, my soul waits,
 and in his word I hope;
my soul waits for the Lord
 more than those who watch for the morning,
 more than those who watch for the morning.

O Israel, hope in the LORD!
 For with the LORD there is steadfast love,
 and with him is great power to redeem.
It is he who will redeem Israel
 from all its iniquities.

—Psalm 130

LENT AND LAPSED TIME

Revelation of God

Mark Link tells the following story:

> A "puzzle page" in the newspaper showed a drawing of an outdoor scene. Beneath it was this question: "Can you find the girl in the drawing?" A close examination of the drawing showed the girl's eyes and eyebrows concealed in a tree branch. Another branch hid her mouth and nose. A cloud revealed her flowing hair. After you discovered the girl, that drawing was never the same again.
>
> —*Vision 2000,* 51

It is like that with God. God is always there in our lives waiting to be found. Once we find him, our picture of the world will never be the same again.

Timing and Patience

For a comedian timing is everything; so too in life. Many imaginative entrepreneurs move too fast only to be faced with a debt-ridden wait. An old Chinese proverb reads:

Patience is power.
With time and patience
the mulberry leaf becomes silk.

LENT AND LAPSED TIME

Order and Chaos in This World

Sometimes it is important that we know where the "boss" is. She can be moving around the plant, or she might be sitting in her office, but when we ask "is everything running properly," we are consoled to hear that the "boss is in her office and able to be reached by her secretary." On a cosmic level (comparing plant with planet), we ask similar questions: "Who is in charge? Is everything okay?"

Robert Browning consoles us in this brief passage from "Pippa Passes":

> **The year's at the spring**
> **And day's at the morn;**
> **Morning's at seven;**
> **The hill-side's dew-pearled;**
> **The lark's on the wing;**
> **The snail's on the thorn;**
> **God's in his heaven—**
> **All's right with the world!**

—Robert Browning

April Prayers

Springing to Life

Our Sacred Land

Spiritually we are all Jews receiving the promise of God to enter a new land and a new life. This will be a land "flowing with milk and honey." The land itself symbolizes God's gifts—hidden and apparent.

The land ties us to all of nature as the gifts of God unfold daily in marvelous yet quite natural ways. We read in Deuteronomy:

> **For the LORD your God is bringing you into a good land, a land with flowing streams, with springs and underground waters welling up in valleys and hills, a land of wheat and barley, of vines and fig trees and pomegranates, a land of olive trees and honey, a land where you may eat bread without scarcity, where you will lack nothing, a land whose stones are iron and from whose hills you may mine copper. You shall eat your fill and bless the LORD your God for the good land that he has given you.**

> —Deuteronomy 8:7-10

SPRINGING TO LIFE

Variety of Gifts

Some of us get carried away with our own unique talents and gifts, until we realize that all of our talents or unique gifts come from God our creator. Paul says:

> Now there are varieties of gifts, but the same Spirit; and there are varieties of services, but the same Lord; and there are varieties of activities, but it is the same God who activates all of them in everyone. To each is given the manifestation of the Spirit for the common good. To one is given through the Spirit the utterance of wisdom, and to another the utterance of knowledge according to the same Spirit, to another faith by the same Spirit, to another gifts of healing by the one Spirit, to another the working of miracles, to another prophecy, to another the discernment of spirits, to another various kinds of tongues, to another the interpretation of tongues. All these are activated by one and the same Spirit, who allots to each one individually just as the Spirit chooses.

> —1 Corinthians 12:4-11

God in Nature

William Wordsworth tells of taking time out to listen to nature as nature speaks of God. He urges us to go out into the untraveled paths of our wonderful atmosphere simply to listen as God speaks to us. Wordsworth says:

> For I have learned
> To look on Nature, not as in the hour
> Of thoughtless youth; but hearing oftentimes
> The still, sad music of humanity,
> Not harsh nor grating, though of ample power
> To chasten and subdue. And I have felt
> A presence that disturbs me with the joy
> Of elevated thoughts; a sense sublime
> Of something far more deeply interfused,
> Whose dwelling is the light of setting suns,
> And the round ocean and the living air,
> And the blue sky, and in the mind of man;
> A motion and a spirit, that impels
> All thinking things, all objects of all thought,
> And rolls through all things.

—William Wordsworth,
"Lines, Composed a Few Miles Above Tintern Abbey . . ."

Mystery of God and Life

Everyone would be pleased to know who God is. This enduring and, at times, overwhelming mystery of God stalks us at every turn in our life's journey. Alfred Tennyson remarks about a very limited and fragile understanding of God through nature that intrigues us. His sensitivity becomes for us a prayer.

> **Flower in the crannied wall,**
> **I pluck you out of the crannies,**
> **I hold you here, root and all, in my hand,**
> **Little flower—but if I could understand**
> **What you are, root and all, and all in all,**
> **I should know what God and man is.**
>
> —Alfred Tennyson, "Flower in the Crannied Wall"

Let us pray silently for a moment that we may accept with greater ease the mystery of God, of our fellow human beings, and of all creatures in this world.

May Prayers

Warm Breath of the Spirit

God, the Unknown

As long as we live, we run the danger of becoming discouraged in our faith. We need support and reinforcement that we do not believe in vain, and that there is a true God guiding us no matter how unknowable this God is. Anthony de Mello gives us a most pleasant story about a bird compelled to sing. He says:

The disciples were full of questions about God.

Said the Master, "God is the Unknown and the Unknowable. Every statement made about Him, every answer to your questions, is a distortion of the Truth." The disciples were bewildered. "Then why do you speak about Him at all?"

"Why does the bird sing?" said the Master.

A bird does not sing because he has a statement. He sings because he has a song.

The words of the Scholar are to be understood. The words of the Master are not to be understood. They are to be listened to as one listens to the wind in the trees and the sound of the river and the song of the bird. They will awaken something within the heart that is beyond all knowledge.

—*The Song of the Bird*, 4–5

Songs of Praise

Sometimes it is beneficial to pray aloud as a community. The ancient prayers of the Jews as well as later Christians allowed for this antiphonal praying. Let us examine a psalm for our prayer today.

Praise the LORD!
Praise God in his sanctuary;
   praise him in his mighty firmament!
Praise him for his mighty deeds;
   praise him according to his surpassing greatness!

Praise him with trumpet sound;
   praise him with lute and harp!
Praise him with tambourine and dance;
   praise him with strings and pipe!
Praise him with clanging cymbals;
   praise him with loud clashing cymbals!
Let everything that breathes praise the LORD!
Praise the LORD!

—Psalm 150

Gentleness

Ralph Waldo Emerson said: "What you are speaks so loudly, I can't hear what you are saying." Jesus taught not only by words but especially by his actions. When we seek advice or consolation from Jesus, we can go to the Scriptures, especially to the following passage:

> **Come to me, all you that are weary and are carrying heavy burdens, and I will give you rest. Take my yoke upon you, and learn from me; for I am gentle and humble in heart, and you will find rest for your souls.**
>
> —Matthew 11:28-29

WARM BREATH OF THE SPIRIT

To Be a Part of Life

Our identity is tied to our surroundings. As citizens of our global village we display certain attitudes and inclinations. We take our past forward and we grow from what we experience. We accept our personal history and the vitality that flows from this history. Alfred Tennyson says:

> **I am a part of all that I have met;**
> **Yet all experience is an arch wherethrough**
> **Gleams that untraveled world, whose margin fades**
> **Forever and forever when I move.**
> **How dull it is to pause, to make an end,**
> **to rust unburnished, not to shine in use!**

—Alfred Tennyson, from "Ulysses"

June Prayers

Summer Splendor Deserving Our Praise

SUMMER SPLENDOR DESERVING OUR PRAISE

God's Grandeur

When we wear shoes we do not feel the various seams and pockets of the ground. We do not feel the difference when we move from dirt to asphalt to cement as we walk forward to our goals. Yet in many places in our world children still run barefoot during the summer. They sensitize their feet to the pebbles and clay and grass and cement that meets them as they move through their vacation days.

Gerard Manley Hopkins sees God's grandeur in this pedestrian experience. Let us reflect the sensitivity we desire for our daily lives as we begin this meeting. Let us ask again for sensitive hearts as we reflect on God's grandeur.

The world is charged with the grandeur of God.
It will flame out, like shining from shook foil;
It gathers to a greatness, like the ooze of oil
Crushed. Why do men then now not reck his rod?
Generations have trod, have trod, have trod;
And all is seared with trade; bleared, smeared
      with toil;
And wears man's smudge and shares man's smell:
      the soil
Is bare now, nor can foot feel, being shod.
And for all this, nature is never spent;
There lives the dearest freshness deep down things;
And though the last lights off the black West went
Oh, morning, at the brown brink eastward,
      springs—
Because the Holy Ghost over the bent
World broods with warm breast and with ah! bright
      wings.

          —Gerard Manley Hopkins, "God's Grandeur"

Love—Compassion—Forgiveness

Tied to love is the virtue of forgiveness. Paul sees God's love for us as a basic motive for developing compassion and patience as we daily interact with our fellow human beings.

As God's chosen ones, holy and beloved, clothe yourselves with compassion, kindness, humility, meekness, and patience. Bear with one another and, if anyone has a complaint against another, forgive each other; just as the Lord has forgiven you, so you also must forgive. Above all, clothe yourselves with love, which binds everything together in a perfect harmony. And let the peace of Christ rule in your hearts, to which indeed you were called in the one body.

—Colossians 3:12-15

Call of Jeremiah as Elemental to All Vocations

Jeremiah reveals how God called him to prophecy and promised special protection during Jeremiah's service. This passage evokes reflection in each of us as we respond to God in our personal vocations to live out our lives.

Now the word of the LORD came to me saying,
  "Before I formed you in the womb I knew you,
  and before you were born I consecrated you;
  I appointed you a prophet to the nations."

Then I said, "Ah, Lord GOD! Truly I do not know how to speak, for I am only a boy." But the LORD said to me,

  "Do not say, 'I am only a boy';
  for you shall go to all to whom I send you,
  and you shall speak whatever I command you.
  Do not be afraid of them,
  for I am with you to deliver you,
          says the LORD."

—Jeremiah 1:4-8

SUMMER SPLENDOR DESERVING OUR PRAISE

Wrestle with God

As Christians and Jews we believe that we are children of Abraham, Isaac, and Jacob. We believe they are our ancestors who historically handed down to us our faith, God-given though it is. Strangely enough, Jacob's name was changed. God changed Jacob's name because one evening Jacob confronted God, talked and debated with God, and eventually wrestled with God. For this reason God changed Jacob's name to Israel, which means "One who wrestles with God." As we read the passage below recounting the story, we can reflect that as children of Jacob, we are Israelites; we have the right to wrestle, spiritually at least, with God. We always keep in mind that each encounter with God is prompted by love and devotion.

The same night he got up and took his two wives, his two maids, and his eleven children, and crossed the ford of the Jabbok. He took them and sent them across the stream, and likewise everything that he had. Jacob was left alone; and a man wrestled with him until daybreak. When the man saw that he did not prevail against Jacob, he struck him on the hip socket; and Jacob's hip was put out of joint as he wrestled with him. Then he said, "Let me go, for the day is breaking." But Jacob said, "I will not let you go, unless you bless me." So he said to him, "What is your name?" And he said, "Jacob." Then the man said, "You shall no longer be called Jacob, but Israel, for you have striven with God and with humans, and have prevailed." Then Jacob asked him, "Please tell me your name." But he said, "Why is it that you ask my name?" And there he blessed him.

—Genesis 32:22-29

July Prayers

Vacations and Leisure

Worry

Psychologists remind us that worry never assists us as we face life's problems. We have at times a need for concern about human obligations and how to fulfill them, but worry and concern are as different as pneumonia and a slight cold.

In the Sermon on the Mount, Matthew highlights the limits of worry in our spiritual life.

Therefore I tell you, do not worry about your life, what you will eat or what you will drink, or about your body, what you will wear. Is not life more than food, and the body more than clothing? Look at the birds of the air; they neither sow nor reap nor gather into barns, and yet your heavenly Father feeds them. Are you not of more value than they? And can any of you by worrying add a single hour to your span of life? And why do you worry about clothing? Consider the lilies of the field, how they grow; they neither toil nor spin, yet I tell you, even Solomon in all his glory was not clothed like one of these. But if God so clothes the grass of the field, which is alive today and tomorrow is thrown into the oven, will he not much more clothe you—you of little faith? Therefore do not worry, saying, "What will we eat?" or "What will we drink?" or "What will we wear?" For it is the Gentiles who strive for all these things; and indeed your heavenly Father knows that you need all these things. But strive first for the kingdom of God and his righteousness, and all these things will be given to you as well.

—Matthew 6:25-33

VACATIONS AND LEISURE

Goodness of God

Sometimes it is difficult to recognize the goodness of God in the face of overwhelming human suffering.

This understanding is expressed in the beautiful but simple prayer of a Breton fisherman who said:

Dear God:
Be good to me:
The sea is so wide,
And my boat is so small.
Amen.

—The Oxford Book of Prayers

VACATIONS AND LEISURE

Truth

The mottoes on the coats of arms of many educational institutions tell of the constant academic search for truth. How often you and I fail to seek out the truth that is in ourselves—our hearts, our personalities. John's Gospel records optimistically:

You will know the truth, and the truth will make you free.

—John 8:32

William Shakespeare many centuries later adds:

This above all
to thine own self be true
And it must follow,
As the night the day
Thou canst not then be false to any man.

—*Hamlet*, act 1, scene 3

VACATIONS AND LEISURE

Perfection—Faith in Christ

We pray to be perfect in God's eyes. Moreover, we pray that we recognize that perfection does not come merely by following laws and rules. Our perfection comes from our faith in God. Paul reviews these ideas in his Letter to the Philippians.

> Yet whatever gains I had, these I have come to regard as loss because of Christ. More than that, I regard everything as loss because of the surpassing value of knowing Christ Jesus as my Lord. For his sake I have suffered the loss of all things, and I regard them as rubbish, in order that I may gain Christ and be found in him, not having a righteousness of my own that comes from the law, but one that comes through faith in Christ, the righteousness from God based on faith.

—Philippians 3:7-9

August Prayers

Honor to Summer Sliding and Serious Planning

Suffering and Joy

It is possible to decrease the suffering in the world by adding to the joy. It is possible to add to the light rather than trying to destroy the darkness. Once you begin to acknowledge random acts of kindness—both the ones you have received and the ones you have given—you can no longer believe that what you do does not matter.

The above quote from *Random Acts of Kindness* brings the word "random" into a new light. We ask ourselves the question: "Are we trained to think only of deficits, notice only people's faults, reflect only on human suffering?"

The Gospels and people who live the Gospels such as Maya Angelou, Mother Teresa, and Pope John XXIII tell us we can and do make a difference. WE CAN DO!

Pure Religion

Regardless of our culture or family background, religion is a most personal issue. For the Jews who so easily could become embroiled in cultural problems, the words of James strike home. Religion is never meant to be a complicated, doctrine-driven experience. In his epistle we read:

Religion that is pure and undefiled before God, the Father, is this: to care for orphans and widows in their distress, and to keep oneself unstained by the world.

—James 1:27

A modern-day Eastern description of religion arises from the Dalai Lama, who says:

My religion is very simple.
My religion is kindness.

—as quoted in *Random Acts of Kindness*, 20

Power, Greed, and Corruption

The ancients tell the story of a great-hearted soul who ran through city streets crying, "Power, greed, and corruption. Power, greed, and corruption." For a time, at least, the attentions of the people were riveted on this single-minded, open-hearted person for whom all of life had become focused on one great question. But then, eventually, everyone went back to work, some only slightly hearing, others clearly annoyed. However, the cries continued: "Power, greed, and corruption. Power, greed, and corruption."

One day a child stepped in front of the wailing figure.

"Elder," said the child, "don't you realize that no one is listening to you?"

"Of course I do, my child," the Elder answered.

"Then why do you shout?" the child inquired as if in disbelief. "If nothing is changing, your efforts are useless."

"Ah, dear child, these efforts are never useless," said the Elder. "You see, I do not shout only in order to change the people, I shout so that they cannot change me."

—Anonymous

Quiet Work

We all want to contribute something lasting to the world. Our desire for immortality is ineluctably linked to our desire to do something that will live on after we die. All-in-all, there is pride and selfishness in this desire, but if it comes as an awareness that we are instruments of God meant to accomplish only what God wills, we fit more humbly in the "scheme of things."

One lesson, Nature, let me learn of thee,
One lesson which in every wind is blown,
One lesson of two duties kept as one
Though the loud world proclaim their enmity—
Of toil unsevered from tranquillity,
Of labor, that in lasting fruit outgrows
Far noisier schemes, accomplished in repose,
Too great for haste, too high for rivalry!

Yes, while on earth a thousand discords ring,
Man's fitful uproar mingling with his toil,
Still do thy sleepless ministers move on,
Their glorious tasks in silence perfecting;
Still working, blaming still our vain turmoil,
Laborers that shall not fail, when man is gone.

—Matthew Arnold, "Quiet Work"

September Prayers

A New Start Toward Fall

A NEW START TOWARD FALL

Love

The simple identity of God and love gives deeper understanding to both words. Yet, each remains mysterious in its transcendent power. As we begin our meeting we reflect on our faith commitment to love one another while we conduct the daily business of our life with one another. The First Letter of John alerts us to the connection between God and love.

Beloved, let us love one another, because love is from God; everyone who loves is born of God and knows God. Whoever does not love does not know God, for God is love.

—1 John 4:7-8

A NEW START TOWARD FALL

The Good Shepherd

I suppose if you asked most ordinary people on the street to recite one psalm they know, they would announce that it is Psalm
23. The institutional Church uses this psalm to console the be-
reaved and the downtrodden, but you and I find personal support in it for all types of experiences of daily living.

> The LORD is my shepherd, I shall not want.
>   He makes me lie down in green pastures;
> he leads me beside still waters;
>   he restores my soul.
> He leads me in right paths
>   for his name's sake.
>
> Even though I walk through the darkest valley,
>   I fear no evil;
> for you are with me;
>   your rod and your staff—
>   they comfort me.
>
> You prepare a table before me
>   in the presence of my enemies;
> you anoint my head with oil;
>   my cup overflows.
> Surely goodness and mercy shall follow me
>   all the days of my life,
> and I shall dwell in the house of the LORD
>   my whole life long.

—Psalm 23

Work Prayer for a Busy Person

As a paraphrase to Psalm 23 the following prayer for a busy person is especially suited to our contemporary societal value system. Now, more than in the past, we are people bent on speed, efficiency, and accomplishment. The slayer lurking in the background is our growing materialistic view of life. We hurry to make money while neglecting to contemplate the riches of nature appreciated only at a pace that is slower than that to which many of us have grown accustomed.

The Lord is my pace-setter. I shall not rush. He makes me stop and rest for quiet intervals. He provides me with images of stillness which restore my serenity. He leads me in ways of efficiency through calmness of mind.

His guidance is peace even though I have a great many things to accomplish. I will not fret, for his presence is here. He prepares refreshment and renewal in the midst of my activities by anointing me with his oils of tranquillity.

My cup of joyous energy overflows. Surely, harmony and effectiveness shall be the fruit of my hours. I shall walk in the peace of the Lord and dwell in his house forever.

—Anonymous

A NEW START TOWARD FALL

Let It Be Forgotten

The discipline of learning how to forget things, events, circumstances is a harsh discipline. Poets and philosophers alike suggest that our life is richer if we learn to forget certain events from the past.

> **Let it be forgotten, as a flower is forgotten,**
> **Forgotten as a fire that once was singing gold,**
> **Let it be forgotten for ever and ever,**
> **Time is a kind friend, he will make us old.**
>
> **If anyone asks, say it was forgotten**
> **Long and long ago,**
> **As a flower, as a fire, as a hushed footfall**
> **In a long-forgotten snow.**

—Sara Teasdale, "Let It Be Forgotten"

October Prayers

Golden Sunsets Before the Harvest Moon

Prayer of St. Francis

The Prayer of St. Francis of Assisi focuses on the role of service. Francis reminds us that our relation to God and to our fellow human beings is preeminently one of service.

Giving is what life is all about according to this remarkable prayer of the founder of Franciscan spirituality. We celebrate his feast on October 4.

> **Lord, make me an instrument of your peace.**
> **Where there is hatred, let me sow love,**
> **Where there is injury, pardon;**
> **Where there is doubt, faith;**
> **Where there is despair, hope;**
> **Where there is darkness, light;**
> **Where there is sadness, joy;**
> **O divine Master, Grant that I may not so much seek**
> **To be consoled, as to console,**
> **To be understood, as to understand**
> **To be loved, as to love,**
> **For it is in giving that we receive;**
> **It is in pardoning that we are pardoned;**
> **It is in dying that we are born to eternal life.**

—St. Francis of Assisi

Inner Peace

Paul the apostle alerts us to the connection between inner peace and a sensitivity to those who are poor. At first glance, the two ideas appear to lack connection. But as we think about it further, the majority of the people on this planet are poor. To dismiss or disregard this majority would take us out of the mainstream of life. For Paul, peace must be found in the center of the mainstream, not on the fringes. We must be where all types of people live and work to note whether or not we practice charity to our neighbors.

Bless those who persecute you; bless and do not curse them. Rejoice with those who rejoice, weep with those who weep. Live in harmony with one another; do not be haughty, but associate with the lowly; do not claim to be wiser than you are. Do not repay anyone evil for evil, but take thought for what is noble in the sight of all. If it is possible, so far as it depends on you, live peaceably with all.

—Romans 12:14-17

GOLDEN SUNSETS BEFORE THE HARVEST MOON

Love as Followers of Christ

So much of life is mere talk, or as they say in politics, rhetoric. The Gospel of John alerts us to be "doers" of faith, not mere talkers.

We know love by this, that he laid down his life for us—and we ought to lay down our lives for one another. How does God's love abide in anyone who has the world's goods and sees a brother or sister in need and yet refuses help?

Little children, let us love, not in word or speech, but in truth and action.

—1 John 3:16-18

Prayer for Conservation

Care among human beings is a mutual enterprise. We help others so that we may hope that they in turn will help us when we are in need. This principle is true also in our relation to the earth as linked to a life of reciprocal esteem.

**Great Spirit,
give us hearts to understand,
never to take
from creation's beauty more than we give,
never to destroy wantonly for the furtherance of
    greed;
never to deny to give our hands for the building of
    earth's beauty;
never to take from her what we cannot use.
Give us hearts to understand that to destroy earth's
    music is to create confusion;
that to wreck her appearance is to blind us to
    beauty;
that to callously pollute her fragrance is to make a
    house of stench;
that as we care for her she will care for us. Amen.**

—United Nations Environmental Sabbath Program,
Earth Prayers, 118

November Prayers

People of God,
All Saints and Sinners Alike

Nature and the Process of Living

Henry Wadsworth Longfellow provides soft, transcendent glimpses of our natural process of living. As if by divine direction at each significant milestone along this path of life nature announces, ever so gently, our current position. In this process nature takes away our playthings in life, one by one, until nothing distracts us from our true purpose for moving along this path.

As a fond mother, when the day is o'er,
　　Leads by the hand her little child to bed,
　　Half willing, half reluctant to be led,
　　And leave his broken playthings on the floor,
Still gazing at them through the open door,
　　Nor wholly reassured and comforted
　　By promises of others in their stead,
　　Which, though more splendid, may not please
　　　　him more;
So Nature deals with us, and takes away
　　Our playthings one by one, and by the hand
　　Leads us to rest so gently, that we go
Scarce knowing if we wish to go or stay,
　　Being too full of sleep to understand
　　How far the unknown transcends what we know.

　　　　　　　　—Henry Wadsworth Longfellow, "Nature"

Thanks

As mysterious as it is, our belief of three persons in One God remains a basic element in our creed. Gratitude to God is always a thanksgiving prayer to the three persons of God: Father, Son, and Holy Spirit. This following community prayer of thanks artfully speaks for all Christians.

For the bread that we have eaten
For the wine that we have tasted
For the life that you have given:
Father, Son and Holy Spirit,
We will praise you.

For the life of Christ within us
Turning all our fears to freedom
Helping us to live for others:
Father, Son and Holy Spirit,
We will praise you.

For the strength of Christ to lead us
In our living and our dying,
In the end with all your people
Father, Son and Holy Spirit,
We will praise you.

—from Contemporary Prayers for Public Worship in
The Oxford Book of Prayers

PEOPLE OF GOD, ALL SAINTS AND SINNERS ALIKE

This Thanksgiving Day

On this Thanksgiving Day as we specifically give thanks for all God's gifts and blessings, we should remember to give thanks and praise to the Lord our God. We are happy to do so not only on this glad day but always and everywhere.

Thankful may I ever be for everything that God bestows.
Thankful for the joys and sorrows, for the blessings and the blows.
Thankful for the wisdom gained through hardships and adversity.
Thankful for the undertones as well as for the melody.

Thankful may I ever be for benefits both great and small
—and never fail in gratitude for that divinest gift of all:
the love of friends that I have known in times of failure and success.
O may the first prayer of the day be always one of thankfulness.

—Patience Strong, excerpts from "This Thanksgiving Day"

PEOPLE OF GOD, ALL SAINTS AND SINNERS ALIKE

Let the Day Come, Lord

Archbishop Oscar Romero wrote several prayers in the last two years of his life before being assassinated in El Salvador. One example is:

> Come, Lord Jesus, come!
> Let the day come, Lord,
>   when our misery
> will find your mercy.
> Let the day come, Lord,
>   when our poverty
> will find your riches.
> Let the day come, Lord,
>   when our path
> will find the way to your house.
> Let the day come, Lord,
>   when our tears
> will find your smile.
> Let the day come, Lord,
>   when our joy
> will find your heaven.
> Let the day come, Lord,
>   when your Church
> will find your Kingdom.
> May you be blest, Father,
>   for that day
> when our eyes will find your face!
> Throughout all the time of our life
> you have not ceased to come before us
>   in your Son Jesus Christ,
> our Savior and our brother.

December Prayers

Advent Life, Messianic Hope

My Gift

Gift giving is a basic custom at Christmas. The obvious danger of going overboard with that aspect of the season looms always in the background. We know that the material aspects of gift giving could do damage to the warm spirit of the custom. We continue to ask: If Christ is the ultimate gift of Christmas, where does our gift giving belong? A poem by Christina Rossetti puts us safely on track during the Christmas season.

What can I give Him
Poor as I am?
If I were a shepherd,
I would give Him a lamb,
If I were a Wise Man,
I would do my part—
But what can I give Him,
Give my heart.

—Christina G. Rossetti, excerpt from "A Christmas Carol"

Christmas

The compelling message of Christmas carries over into the new year. The following prayer repeats the Christmas challenge to each of us as we celebrate this feast of light and life.

> **When the song of the angels is stilled;**
> **When the star in the sky is gone;**
> **When the kings and priests are home;**
> **When the shepherds are back with their flocks. . . .**
> **The work of Christmas begins. . . .**
> **To find the lost,**
> **To heal the broken,**
> **To feed the hungry,**
> **To release the prisoner,**
> **To rebuild the nations,**
> **To bring peace among peoples. . . .**
> **To make music in the heart!**

ADVENT LIFE, MESSIANIC HOPE

Christmas

God's glory, now, is kindled, gentler than low
    candlelight
Under the rafters of a barn.
Eternal Peace is sleeping in the hay,
And wisdom's born in secret in a straw-roofed
    stable.
And O! Make holy music in the stars, you happy
    angels;
You shepherds, gather on the hill.

—Thomas Merton, "Carol"

Christmas

Robert Louis Stevenson reflects on the meaning of Christmas that flows from the Gospel story:

O God, our loving Father, help us rightly to remember the birth of Jesus, that we may share in the song of the angels, the gladness of the shepherds, the worship of the wise men. Close the door to hate, and open the door of love all over the world. Let kindness come with every gift and good desires with every greeting. Deliver us from evil by the blessing that Christ brings, and teach us to be merry with clean hearts. May the Christmas morning make us happy to be thy children and the Christmas evening bring us to our beds with grateful thoughts, forgiving and forgiven, for Jesus' sake. Amen.

—Robert Louis Stevenson

Prayers for the End
of Meetings

Prayer

St. Benedict used a famous maxim as a central support to the entire Benedictine life: "pray and work" *(ora et labora)*. Strangely enough, the simple coordinating conjunction is pivotal to this statement, and is used to show an equal balance between what went before and what follows. Prayer alone or work alone is insufficient. St. Ignatius said it another way:

Work as though all depends on you.
Pray as though all depends on God.

Gaelic Blessing

In gift shops around the world we find this Irish blessing that speaks the heart of all nationalities.

May the road rise to meet you.
May the wind be always at your back.
May the sun shine warm upon your face.
May the rains fall softly upon your fields.
And until we meet again,
May God hold you in the hollow of his hand.

—"Old Gaelic Blessing,"
excerpted from *The Oxford Book of Prayers*

The Lord's Prayer

When Hollywood discovered that it could use slow motion in films to heighten dramatic effect, a whole new way of directing films evolved.

When you and I pray, often we realize we must first slow down to open our hearts to the effects God wishes to produce. For a change of pace let us recite together the Our Father, but let us say it ever so slowly, pausing slightly after each phrase. Allow me to lead this prayer and set the pace. Please chime in.

**Our Father, who art in heaven,
hallowed be thy name;
Thy kingdom come;
Thy will be done on earth as it is in heaven.
Give us this day our daily bread;
and forgive us our trespasses
as we forgive those who trespass against us;
and lead us not into temptation,
but deliver us from evil.
For the kingdom, the power and the glory are
     yours,
now and forever. Amen.**

God's Love

St. Augustine reminds us that God is closer and more intimate to us than we are to ourselves. Isaiah 43 reminds us of our place in God's love.

Do not fear, for I have redeemed you;
    I have called you by name, you are mine. . . .
You are precious in my sight,
    and honored, and I love you. . . .
Do not fear, for I am with you.

—Isaiah 43:1, 4, 5

Prayers in Anticipation of a Critical Meeting

Oh Yet We Trust

Two young women were talking—an optimist and a pessimist. The optimist said: "This is the best possible world!" The pessimist replied: "I am afraid that you are correct!"

You and I fit into one or the other position, but with a sense of God in our lives, the world makes more sense. Below are some thoughts by Alfred Tennyson about our world.

Oh yet we trust that somehow good
  Will be the final goal of ill,
  To pangs of nature, sins of will,
Defects of doubt, and taints of blood;

That nothing walks with aimless feet;
  That not one life shall be destroyed,
  Or cast as rubbish to the void,
When God hath made the pile complete;

That not a worm is cloven in vain;
  That not a moth with vain desire
  Is shriveled in a fruitless fire,
Or but subserves another's gain.

Behold, we know not anything;
  We can but trust that good shall fall
  At last—far off—at last, to all
And every winter change to spring.

So runs my dream; but what am I?
  An infant crying in the night:
  An infant crying for the light:
And with no language but a cry.

—Alfred Tennyson, "Oh Yet We Trust"

Humility

Pride is a constant, subtle force that silently rusts away our spiritual strength. G. K. Chesterton offers the following prayer as a check to this subtle force.

O God of earth and altar,
   Bow down and hear our cry;
Our earthly rulers falter,
   Our people drift and die;
The walls of gold entomb us,
   The swords of scorn divide,
Take not thy thunder from us,
   But take away our pride.

From all that terror teaches,
   From lies of tongue and pen,
From all the easy speeches
   That comfort cruel men,
From sale and profanation
   Of honor and the sword,
From sleep and from damnation,
   Deliver us, good Lord!

—G. K. Chesterton, "Deliver Us, Good Lord," excerpted from
The Oxford Book of Prayers

Attitude

The brief paragraph "Attitude" shows us the psychological priority of this word among other indicators of virtue and character. Charles Swindoll says:

The longer I live, the more I realize the impact of attitude on life. Attitude, to me, is more important than facts. It is more important than the past, than education, than money, than circumstances, than failures, than successes, than what other people think or say or do. It is more important than appearance, giftedness or skill. It will make or break a company . . . a church . . . a home. The remarkable thing is we have a choice every day regarding the attitude we will embrace for that day. We cannot change our past . . . we cannot change the fact that people will act in a certain way. We cannot change the inevitable. The only thing we can do, is play on the one string we have, and that is our attitude. . . . I am convinced that life is 10 percent what happens to me and 90 percent how I react to it. And so it is with you . . . we are in charge of our ATTITUDES.

The Devil and His Friend

Like the search for truth, the search for a religious truth is an unending journey. This search moves us to the humble conviction that we are never more than pilgrims on a long journey to heaven, the place of full truth. Anthony de Mello says:

The devil once went for a walk with a friend. They saw a man ahead of them stoop down and pick up something from the road.

"What did that man find?" asked the friend.

"A piece of Truth," said the devil.

"Doesn't that disturb you?" asked the friend.

"No, it does not," said the devil, "I shall allow him to make a religious belief out of it."

A religious belief is a signpost pointing the way to Truth. People who cling tenaciously to the signpost are prevented from moving toward the Truth because they have the false feeling that they already possess it.

—*The Song of the Bird*, 46–7

A Candle

The craft of making candles is lost to most of us. Museum and Renaissance fairs remind us of this ancient practice, but we forget that even today, we, on occasion, have need of candles for light. The unknown author below compares the making of a candle with our individual spiritual life.

A candle's but a simple thing,
It starts with just a bit of string.
But dipped and dipped with patient hand
It gathers wax upon the strand
Until complete and snowy white
It gives at last a lovely light.
Life seems so like that bit of string,
Each deed we do a simple thing
Yet day by day if on life's strand
We work with patient heart and hand
It gathers joy, makes Dark days bright
And gives at last a lovely light.

—Anonymous, "A Candle"

The Proper Time

Both the English and the Italians have one rich word in common: "proper" or *"proprio."* This word evokes a warm response from the human emotions in our hearts. We admit, then deny, that this is the proper time. What is difficult or seemingly negative, we avoid; yet it may be the proper time, such as death. What is easy and joyful we readily embrace, knowing that this joy, although proper and appropriate, is passing and limited regardless how meaningful and significant to our total life at the moment. Slowly we repeat these words of the preacher Qoheleth.

For everything there is a season, and a time for every matter under heaven:
   a time to be born, and a time to die;
   a time to plant, and a time to pluck up what is planted;
   a time to kill, and a time to heal;
   a time to break down, and a time to build up;
   a time to weep, and a time to laugh;
   a time to mourn, and a time to dance;
   a time to throw away stones, and a time to gather stones together;
   a time to embrace, and a time to refrain from embracing;
   a time to seek, and a time to lose;
   a time to keep, and a time to throw away;
   a time to tear, and a time to sew;
   a time to keep silence, and a time to speak;
   a time to love, and a time to hate;
   a time for war, and a time for peace.

—Ecclesiastes 3:1-8

Index

The subject references will indicate in parentheses in which month or section a corresponding prayer appears, followed by a page number where the prayer can be found.